—COMPANION GUIDE—

HOW TO FINANCE THE SALE

— A COMPANION TO —

THINK, ACT, BREATHE GLOBAL

By Vernon Darko

Copyright ©2011 by Vernon D. Darko

P.O. Box 890131

Houston, TX 77289

Tel: 281.286.1338. | Fax: 281.286.2825

www.vernondarko.com

ISBN: 978-1-933497-22-8

Printed and bound in the
United States of America

TABLE OF CONTENTS

DISCLAIMER

The information presented herein represents the view of the author as of the date of publication. Due to the rate at which conditions change, the author reserves the right to alter and update his opinion based on new conditions. While every attempt has been made to verify the information in this report, neither the author nor his affiliates/partners assume any responsibility for errors, inaccuracies or omissions. The book is for informational purposes only.

For more information please see the website at http://vernondarko.com

INTRODUCTION

With the book *Think, Act, Breathe Global,* I introduced you to the benefits of going global as well as gave you valuable advice on how to accomplish this, step by step. However, there is one aspect to going global that can be particularly tricky and that is the portion that requires working capital to get your product to market overseas. If you have to finance the entire endeavor yourself, you may need quite the bank roll or pre payment for goods. Neither option is ideal so it is necessary to instead finance the sale.

Luckily there are many different ways this can be accomplished but if you are not familiar with the world of global trade, you may find this step a bit tricky. This is why I have compiled this bonus companion book. In this book I take the available financing options and make them easy to understand so you can determine which one will be best for you.

There are also various risks involved in the transactions so these will be explained at the onset so you have a clear understanding of what may ho wrong in certain situations and what to do about it.

With this companion book you will learn:

- The risks involved with selling to a customer overseas

- The different types of financing options

- Explanations of what each option entails and when to use it

- Products that are eligible for financing

- Collecting payment

- Insuring goods and payments

- Government financing assistance options

- Exploring the Export-Import Bank

With all the information available in this book you will get a complete explanation of the financing options in order to make financing the sale a lot less cumbersome. You will have all this information available at your fingertips to get you started quickly. If you have already read Think, Act, Breathe Global then this will be an invaluable source of additional information. You are ready to get started on your journey toward taking your product global.

Risks Involved With Global Selling

CHAPTER 1.

As with any business venture there are various forms of risks involved. However, with selling products overseas, there are some unique challenges that occur. Your responsibility, as a successful business person is to mitigate these risks as much as possible. The two types of risks are Commercial Risks and Political Risks.

Commercial Risk

Commercial risks can occur with any transaction, global or not. If you extend credit to a customer you run the risk of failing to collect payment. Any type of financial difficulty the buyer is experiencing could jeopardize your odds of getting paid. This may even included bankruptcy; which will make it nearly impossible for you to get your money and will restrict your ability to attempt collections.

You, as the seller, may also run into financial difficulty which could prevent you from delivering the goods to the buyer, thus putting you in a position of losing a customer or even your business. Financial difficulty in your business is not the sole reason, though, for not being able to deliver your goods or to deliver in a timely manner. As we discussed in Think, Act, Breathe Global and Grow Your Business, it is very important to have a supporting group of companies. However, if one of the companies you depend on to manufacture or ship your goods has a problem, it becomes your problem as well. This is why it is important to diversify and ensure backups if needed.

Commercial risks are the most prevalent risks you will run into and not entirely unique to going global.

Political Risk

Political risks are also a possibility and this situation is unique to trading overseas. The government may step in and prevent the trade transaction from completing, which is called Martial Law. It may be that the government prevents the buyer from paying, or it may be that the government restricts, even without prior notice, shipments into the country therefore disallowing delivery of your goods.

Therefore, because of the possible commercial and political risks, it is important to understand the transactions and recognize any implications in trading and how these risks could affect financing. There are a few common ways that financing occurs between the buyer and seller of a global transaction. Letters of credit are the most common and one of the safer means of establishing credit. However, you can also issue open account terms to a buyer.

Notes

_____

_____

_____

_____

_____

_____

_____

_____

_____

_____

_____

_____

_____

_____

_____

_____

_____

_____

_____

_____

_____

Letters Of Credit (Lc)

CHAPTER 2.

A letter of credit is an instrument issued by a bank on behalf of the buyer or importer, in favor of a seller or exporter, promising payment upon presentation of documents. There is a specific documentation requirement that must be met prior to the funds being released. The importer's credit is used to secure the letter of credit and the exporter will receive payment after specific requirements are met. Letters of credit are also available in transferable and back to back LC's:

■ **Transferable**

A transferable LC is an export letter of credit that may be transferred in whole or in part to another beneficiary or supplier.

■ **Back to Back**

Back to back LC's are where one letter of credit is used as collateral to secure another LC to the supplier.

Collecting on a Letter of Credit

Documents against payment, is a payment process, where a sight draft and documents are sent by the exporter (or their bank) to an overseas collecting bank. Documents are then released upon payment to the collecting bank. It is important that the collection form be properly completed and the documents presented with the sight draft. This is a deferred payment option whereby you carry the receivable on your books while awaiting the payment promised by the bank. When the bank accepts the goods the payment is made.

Notes

Open Account Terms

CHAPTER 3.

This is where you simply ship the goods to the buyer and wait to get paid upon receipt of the goods. However, there is no guarantee that you will be paid and this is the most risky way to conduct business, especially if you do not already have a solid working relationship with the buyer. Sometimes extending open credit is a valuable way to establish or strengthen an existing relationship. However, you have to do so carefully so you do not end up with a receivable on your books for an extended period of time without payment.

In order to mitigate some of the risk for issuing open account terms to a buyer, you will want to consider insurance. Without insurance you will have no simple recourse to collect the money that is due to you. However, insurance on the product and financing will reduce some of the risk and guarantee payment even if the receipt of goods is defaulted on.

Should your goods be damaged, stolen or destroyed during shipping, you will receive a payment from the insurance company. This may cover your costs or your costs plus what you would have paid had they all sold at retail price. It depends on the insurance and how much you are willing to pay. The second type of insurance that any exporter should carry is insurance to insure the financing. Even if, on your end, you are essentially paying cash for the goods; it is possible to be covered should the goods, or your company in the destination country, be seized or otherwise taken over because of political reasons or unrest.

Notes

Exploring Government Financing Assistance

CHAPTER 4.

Often countries will provide incentives and assistance in financing since the governments of both the importer and exporter want to encourage economic stability. This helps both countries to ensure a rich business climate and prosperous economy. Check with export assistance centers, the Department of Commerce and the SBA (Small Business Administration). However, the Ex-Im Bank is often the most valuable source of financing for exporters in the U.S.

The Ex-Im bank is an Export/Import bank that was established in 1934 as an independent agency of the government of the United States. It is headquartered in Washington, DC and has eight sales offices to support U.S. exports in order to create and sustain U.S. jobs. There are several trade finance programs that are offered by the Ex-Im Bank including:

■ Domestic Pre-export working capital that can include foreign accounts receivable financing

■ Domestic Post-export Foreign Receivable Financing

■ Foreign Buyer Short-Term Buyer Credit Financing

■ Foreign Buyer Medium-Term and Long-Term Financing via insurance/guarantee programs

Domestic Financing

For domestic financing the borrower is the exporter. In order to be eligible for this program the exporter must have at least 50% U.S. content or added value. For pre-export financing this covers the risk of the exporter's performance and is a working capital guarantee. Advance rates up to 90% are available and pre-sold merchandise is available for an advance rate up to 75%. This program covers 90% of the loan's principal and accrued interest.

Post-export financing includes export credit insurance. This protects the exporter against foreign buyer commercial and political risk as discussed in the first section of this book. It covers 95% commercial and 100% political risk on the financed accounts receivable. Advance rates are available up to 95%.

Some benefits of pre and post-export financing include:

- Expands international sales and market share

- Expands collateral base

- Allows customer to obtain supplier discounts

- Improves cash flow

- Mitigates foreign commercial and political risks for the exporter and/or the bank

Domestic Financing Examples

The process of using the Ex-Im bank may seem a bit confusing but it helps to consider examples of how pre and post-domestic financing works in a practical setting. Consider the following examples:

- Domestic Working Capital Guarantee

An exporter of automotive parts is trying to grow its business by expanding its product lines and entering new foreign markets that Ex-Im Bank is open to. The company needs working capital to maintain inventory and attract buyers by extending sales terms. A Working Capital Guarantee supported by Ex-Im Bank is the solution. With the guarantee, the bank set up a $650M line of credit supported by export inventory and foreign receivables.

- Domestic Export Credit Insurance

A company is engaged in water purification and recycling projects in a country that Ex-Im Bank is open to and is financing its customers by carrying foreign receivables on its books. They also want to expand their business but do not have working capital to do so. The company needs to finance foreign receivables and would like to extend more attractive terms to foreign buyers. An Export Credit Insurance Policy through Ex-Im Bank is the ideal solution. With a policy assignment to the bank, a $4M working capital line of credit is set up.

Foreign Financing

With foreign financing the foreign importer is the borrower of the funds. There are short term, medium term and long term financing options available. A short term financing solution would involve a revolving line of credit that has repayment terms up to 360 days. This type of financing is available for consumer durable goods, bulk agricultural and capital goods with 50% U.S. content or added value. It covers up to 98% of commercial and political risk.

Eligible products for short term buyer financing include:

- Agricultural commodities such as grains, soy bean, rice etc

- Capital goods equipment such as agricultural, fishing & forestry equipment

- Consumer durables

- Raw materials

Medium to long term financing is also available in the form of a term loan for up to seven years with a maximum of $10M. Capital goods and related services are eligible for this type of financing. The total level of support for a supply contract will be the lesser of 85% of the value of all eligible goods and services in the U.S. supply contract; or 100% of the U.S. content in all eligible goods and services in the U.S. supply contract.

Eligible products for foreign buyer medium/long term financing include:

- Agricultural, fishing & forestry equipment

- Communication, telecommunication, sound, image reproduction equipment & systems

- Construction equipment

- Power generating & transmission equipment

- Manufacturing equipment

- Mining extraction & refining equipment

- Industrial machinery

- Transportation equipment

- Office equipment

Benefits of using foreign buyer financing include:

- Improves cash flow for both the importer and exporter

- Reduces foreign commercial and political risks for the exporter and the bank

- Increases competitive position by financing at interest rates that are lower than what is available in most foreign countries

Foreign Financing Examples

Consider the following foreign financing examples:

- Short Term Buyer Credit (FIBC)

A buyer of wheat, rice and other agricultural commodities in a country that Ex-Im Bank is open to, has an opportunity to expand sales of U.S. sourced goods. The company would like to obtain short term working capital financing for U.S. purchases, giving them time to sell the product and minimize the impact on their own cash flow. The solution is a $4M Short Term Buyer Credit (FIBC), with a guarantee provided by Ex-Im Bank. This allows funding of sales to U.S. suppliers with 180 day payment terms to the buyer.

- Medium/Long Term Buyer Credit

A naval unit in a country that Ex-Im Bank is open to wants to buy two new ships to strengthen drug interdiction and reduce illegal immigration. They also want to refurbish four existing ships for the same purpose. The total cost of the project is $26M. This government entity is interested in financing and the U.S. supplier does not have the capacity to extend financing under its own facilities. The solution is a Medium Term Guarantee from Ex-Im Bank allowing 5 year financing for this project directly to the foreign buyer.

Forfaiting

Forfaiting is the discounting of international trade receivables on a non-recourse basis. This type of financing can range from a few months to up to seven years but typically ranges between three and five years. Sums involved may range from a few hundred thousand to millions of dollars. The pricing is usually on a fixed rate basis, and is based on the country and foreign bank risk. The purpose of forfaiting is to convert a term sale into a cash transaction and improve cash flow. Forfaiting is available with 100% financing and no U.S. content requirement.

Notes

Notes

Financing Needs Summary

CHAPTER 7.

Now that you have a good idea of the various types of financing available to fund your sale of goods or services overseas to a global market; let's recap the needs of the exporter:

■ Assess and address your working capital needs

■ Meet with your bank to explore your financing options

■ Explore Letter of Credit tools

■ Explore government assistance programs

- *Export Assistance Centers/Department of Commerce*

- *Small Business Administration (SBA)*

- *Export Import Bank of the U.S. (Ex-Im Bank)*

- *Financing for the exporter or the foreign buyer*

■ Consider Credit Insurance

■ Explore Discounting Receivables

Notes

Ensuring that you have enough working capital to conduct business is essential to going global. You have several options available to you through private banks, export assistance centers and government programs. Explore all the options available to you in order to make a sound decision that will work best for your particular business model.

Use this guide as a companion to Think, Act, Breathe Global and Grow Your Business and you will be well on your way to bringing your product to the world and greatly expanding your client base. With the knowledge you gain from this book you can talk intelligently to banks and government agencies that will assist you in getting your goods or services exported to foreign countries.

I believe it is important for companies to avoid limiting themselves to the United States when selling products. After all, the U.S. comprises just a fraction of the world's population. To limit the country you sell to, limits your potential for profit also. So, now you have all the tools you need to remove this restriction and go global. I wish you luck in your endeavors and I am confident you will succeed in your business venture going global!

If you have any additional questions or want more information, please refer to my website at http://vernondarko.com.

Notes

Notes

Notes

Notes

Notes

Notes

_____

_____

_____

_____

_____

_____

_____

_____

_____

_____

_____

_____

_____

_____

_____

_____

_____

_____

_____

_____

_____

_____

_____

_____

_____

_____

_____

_____